T.L.C.
Transition Leaning Center
2485 Dolan Way
San Pablo, CA 94506

W9-AVA-162

Twizzlers™

Shapes and Patterns

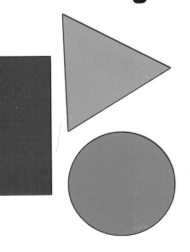

by Jerry Pallotta
Illustrated by Rob Bolster

Cartwheel
·B·O·O·K·S·®
SCHOLASTIC INC.

New York   Toronto   London   Auckland   Sydney   Mexico City   New Delhi   Hong Kong   Buenos Aires

Thank you to Carol Levine.
—— *Jerry Pallotta*

This book is dedicated to Michael Milan.
—— *Rob Bolster*

SHAPES AND PATTERNS AHEAD. HARD HATS REQUIRED BEYOND THIS POINT.

HARD HATS

Copyright © 2002 Hershey Foods Corporation. Trademarks used under license, Corporate Board Books Inc., Licensee.

HERSHEY'S OFFICIAL LICENSED PRODUCT

Text copyright © 2002 by Jerry Pallotta.
Illustrations copyright © 2002 by Rob Bolster.
All rights reserved. Published by Scholastic Inc.
SCHOLASTIC, CARTWHEEL BOOKS, and associated logos
are trademarks and/or registered trademarks of Scholastic Inc.

No part of this publication may be reproduced, or stored in a retrieval system, or transmitted in any form or by any means, electronic, mechanical, photocopying, recording, or otherwise, without written permission of the publisher. For information regarding permission, write to Scholastic Inc., Attention: Permissions Department, 557 Broadway, New York, NY 10012.

Library of Congress Cataloging-in-Publication Data available

ISBN 0-439-34053-5

10 9 8 7 6 5 4 3 2 1   02 03 04 05 06

Printed in U.S.A.   08
This edition first printing, September 2002

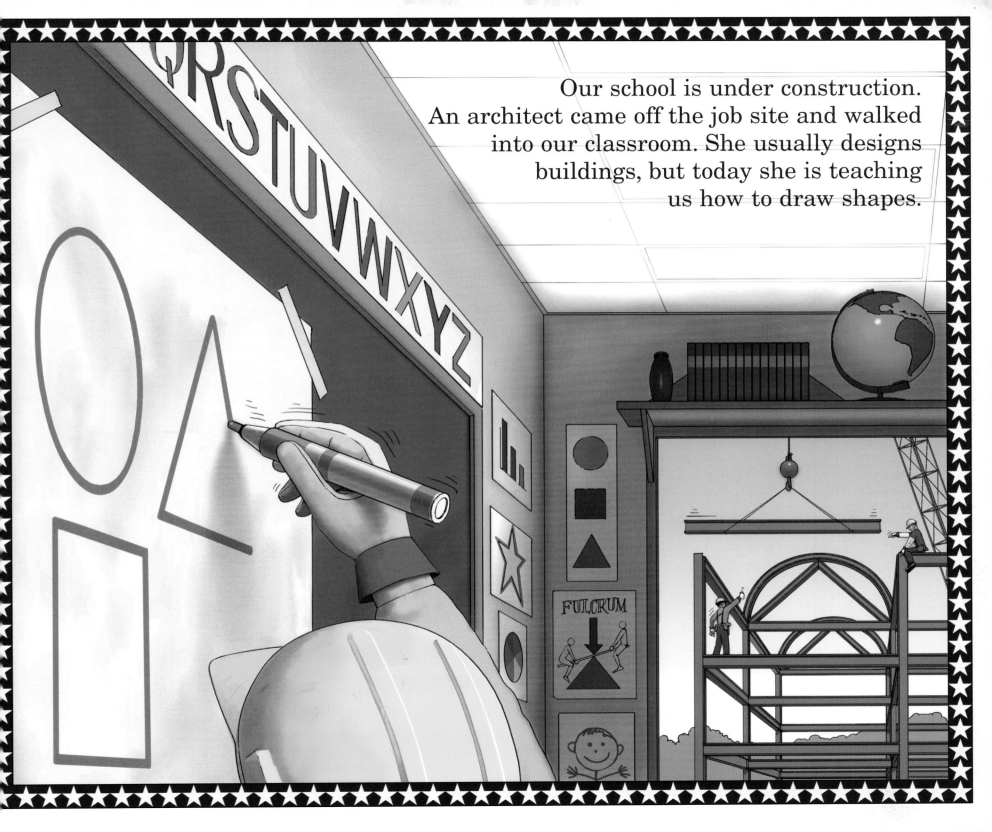

Our school is under construction. An architect came off the job site and walked into our classroom. She usually designs buildings, but today she is teaching us how to draw shapes.

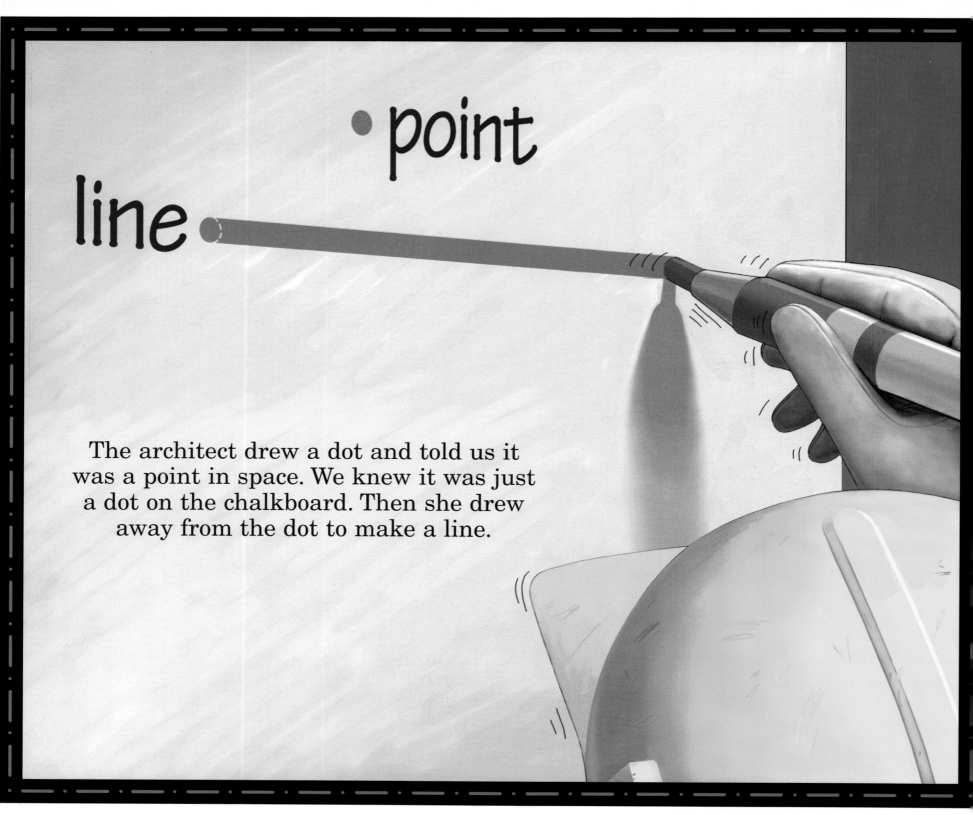

point

line

The architect drew a dot and told us it was a point in space. We knew it was just a dot on the chalkboard. Then she drew away from the dot to make a line.

During the lesson, our teacher gave the whole class a snack. It was TWIZZLERS® Twists! Yeah! Right away I decided to use my strawberry twist as a line.

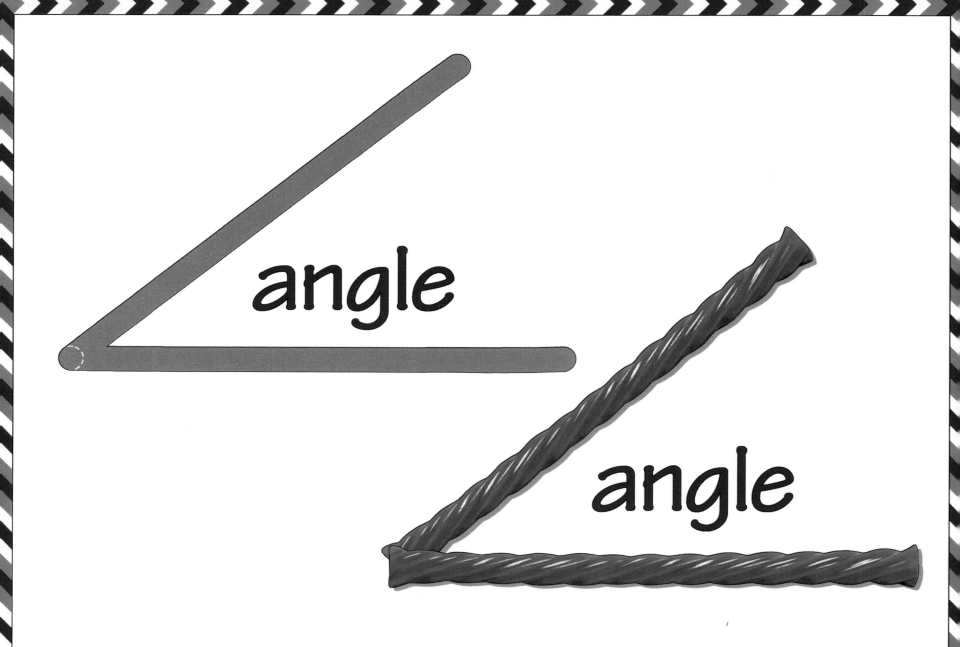

The architect drew another straight line.
She showed us how to make an angle.

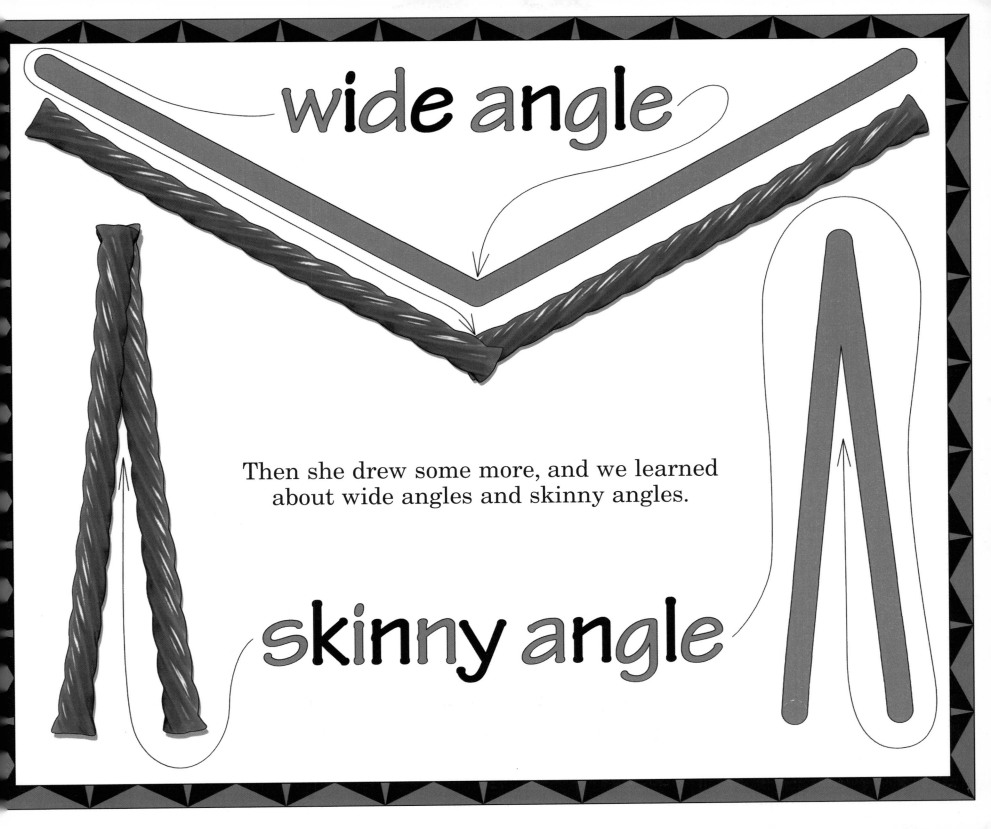

wide angle

Then she drew some more, and we learned about wide angles and skinny angles.

skinny angle

triangle

The first shape the architect showed us was a triangle. It has three sides and three angles. I made a triangle with three strawberry TWIZZLERS candies. It was really fun. I love to learn!

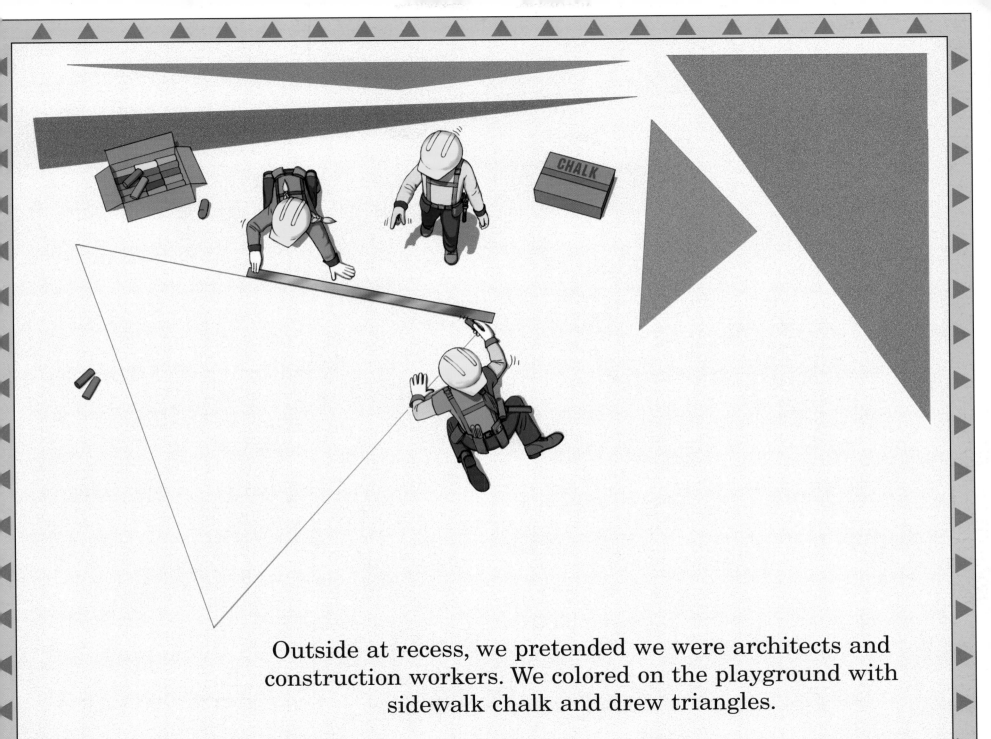

Outside at recess, we pretended we were architects and construction workers. We colored on the playground with sidewalk chalk and drew triangles.

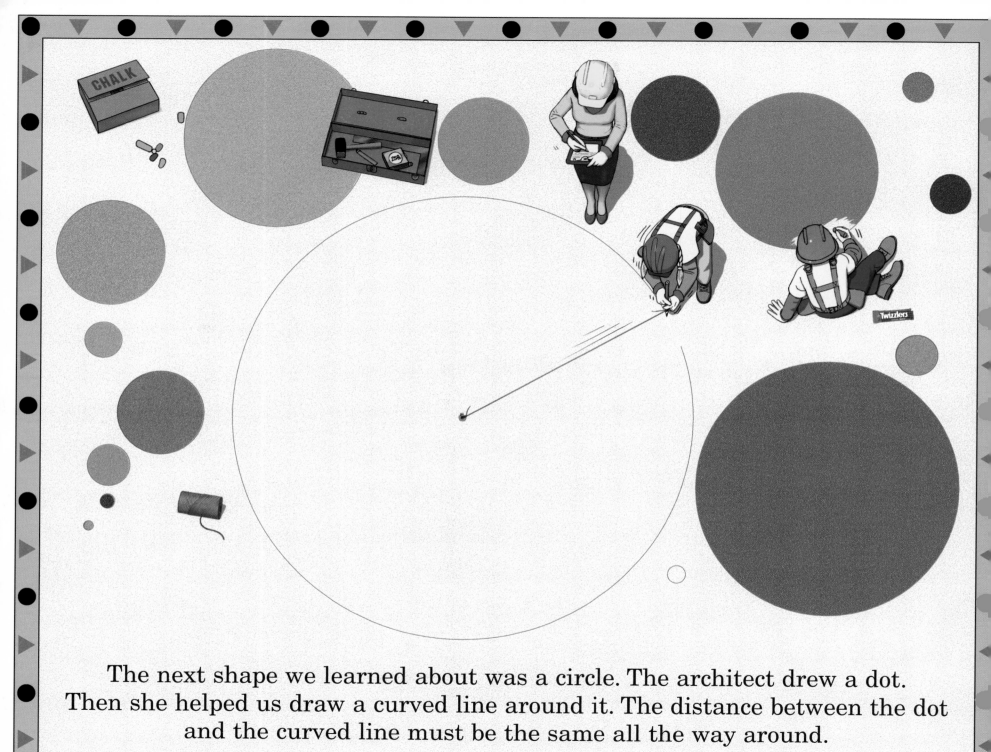

The next shape we learned about was a circle. The architect drew a dot. Then she helped us draw a curved line around it. The distance between the dot and the curved line must be the same all the way around.

circle

My classmate made a circle with licorice.

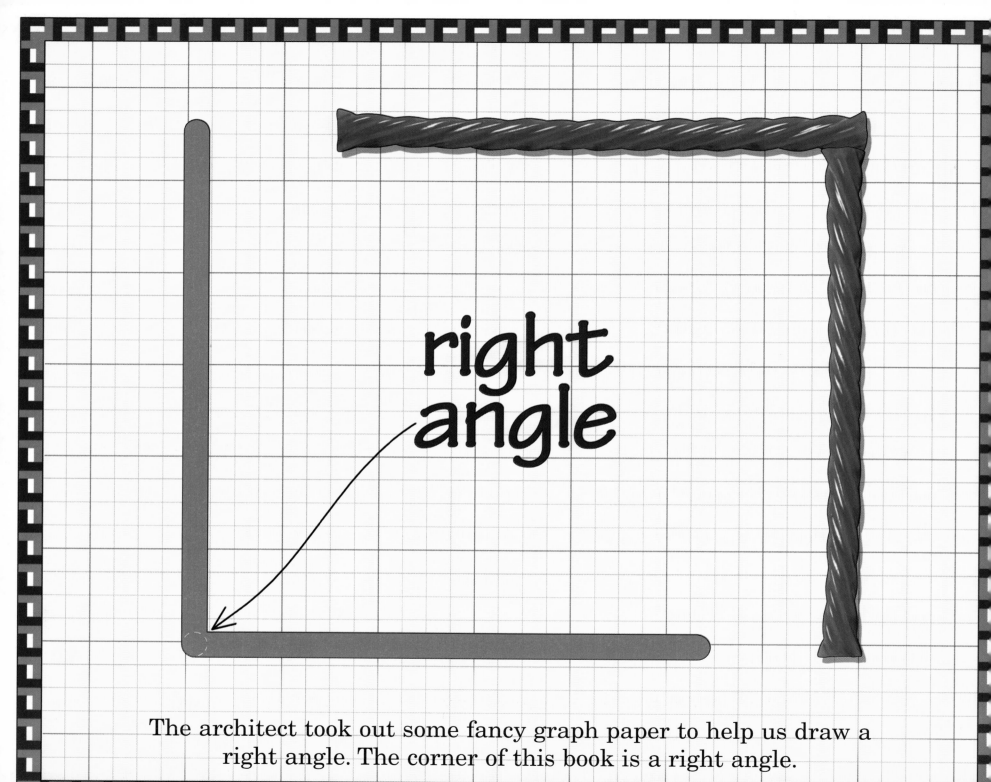

right angle

The architect took out some fancy graph paper to help us draw a right angle. The corner of this book is a right angle.

parallel lines

Lines that are the same distance from each other and do not touch are called parallel lines.

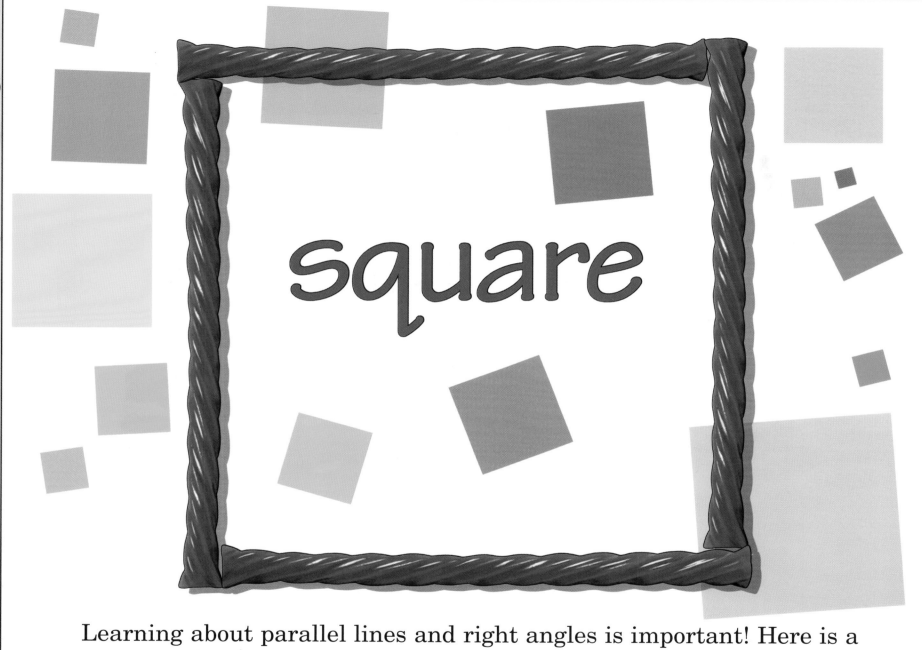

square

Learning about parallel lines and right angles is important! Here is a square. A square is a four-sided shape. All four sides are the same length. All four angles are right angles.

Out on the playground, we tried to trick our teacher. One of the squares that we drew was not really a square. Can you figure out which one is different?

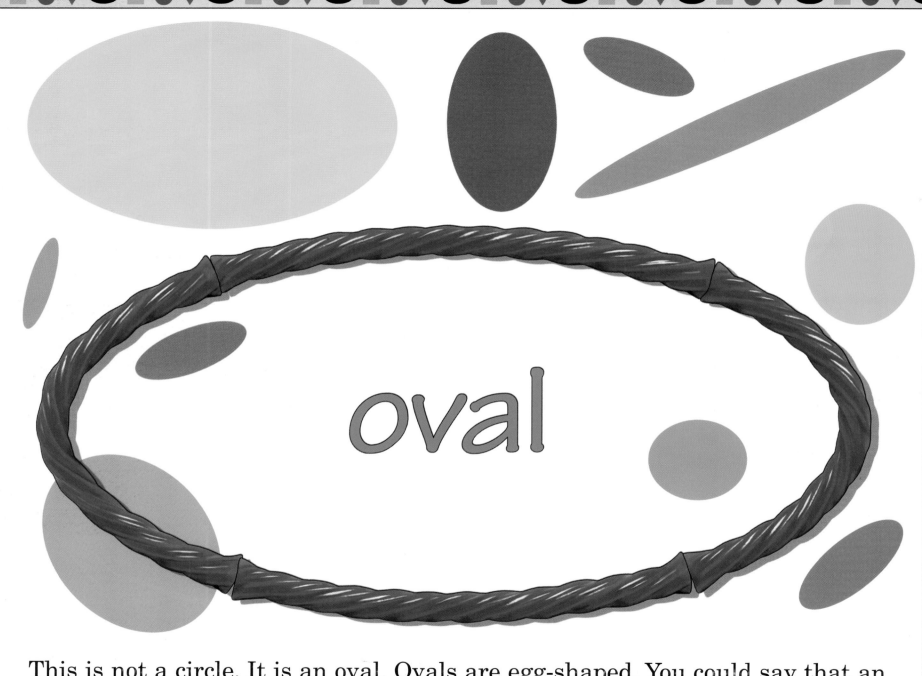

oval

This is not a circle. It is an oval. Ovals are egg-shaped. You could say that an oval looks like a circle that has been stretched or squished.

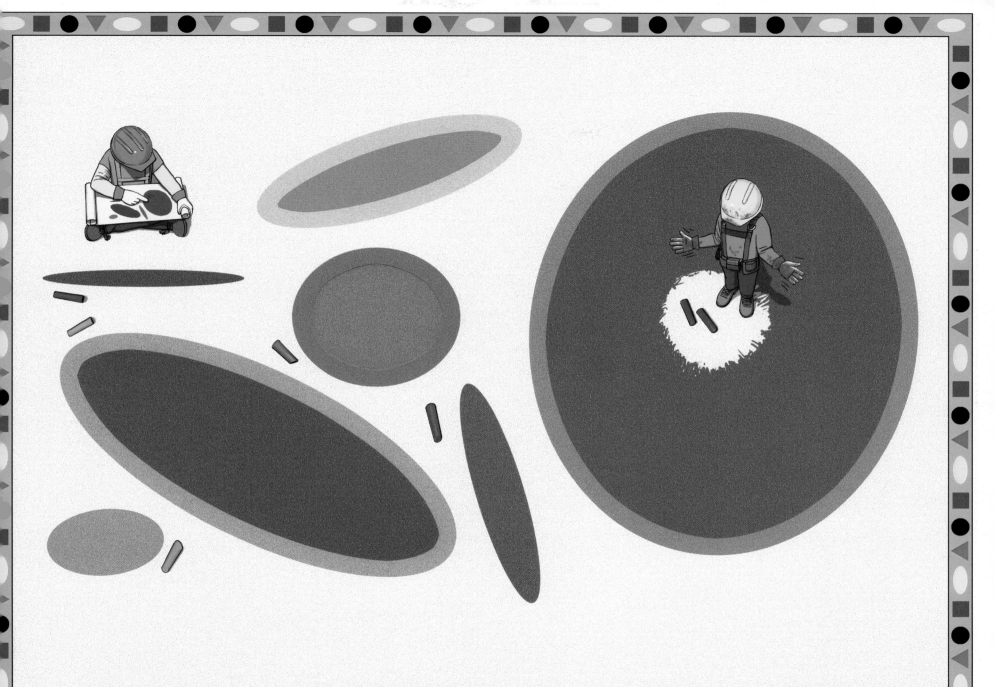

Race cars drive on oval-shaped tracks. The jogging tracks around football fields are oval-shaped. Can you think of other ovals?

rectangle

Rectangles are everywhere. The architect told us to look at doors and windows. A rectangle has four straight lines and four right angles just like a square—but only the two lines opposite each other are the same length.

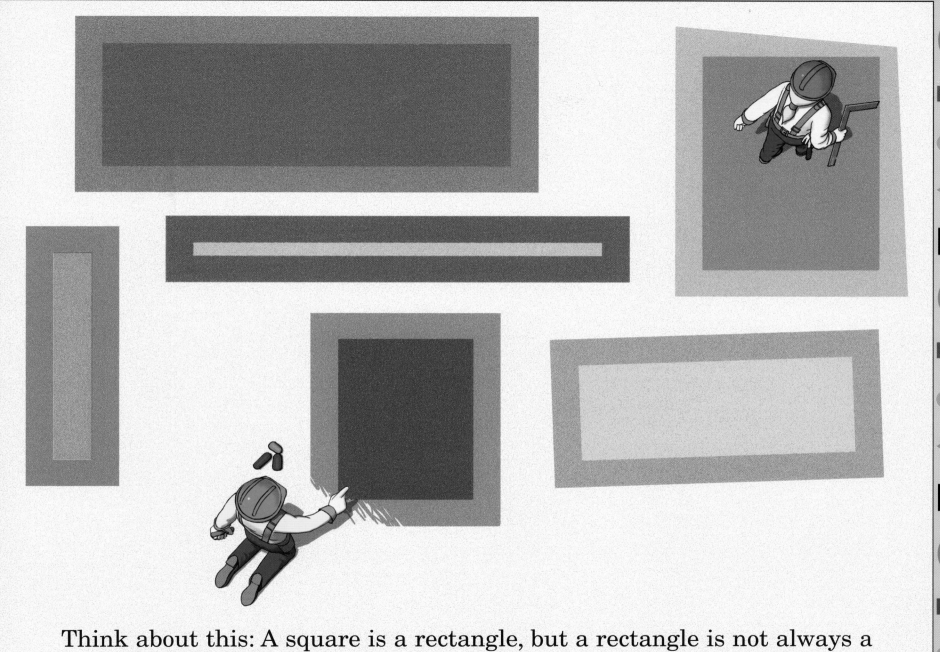

Think about this: A square is a rectangle, but a rectangle is not always a square. Our class could not decide which type is their favorite — short, fat rectangles or really long, skinny rectangles.

A shape with five sides is called a pentagon. This pentagon has five equal sides and five equal angles.

Here is a diamond, a home plate, a kite, and an "I-don't-know-what-to-call-it!" These are polygons. A shape with straight lines and more than three sides is a polygon. The crescent moon and the heart are shapes, too. But they are not polygons. They have curved lines.

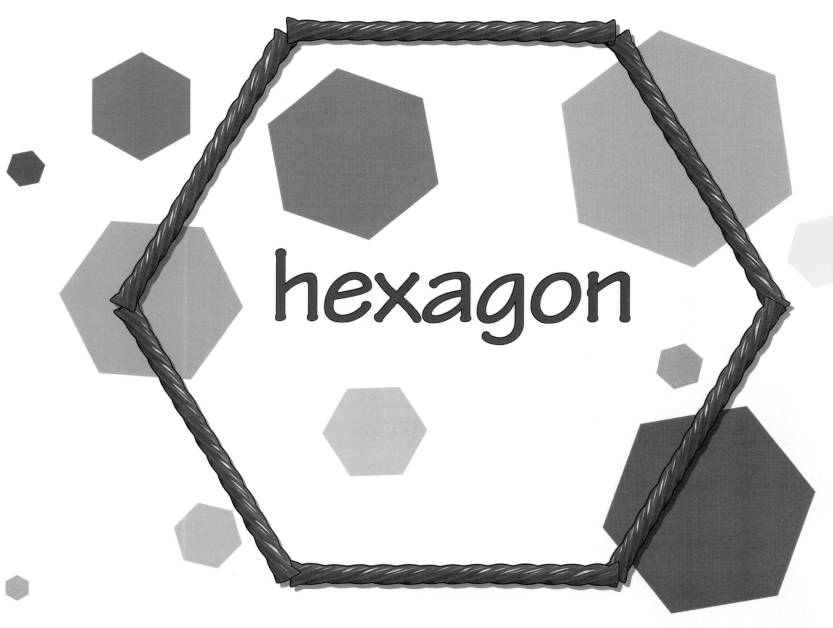

Count the sides of this shape. One, two, three, four, five, six. Now count the angles. One, two, three, four, five, six. This polygon is called a hexagon.

heptagon

The architect let me work on her laptop computer.
We all drew a heptagon just like the one I saw on the computer screen.
A heptagon has seven sides.

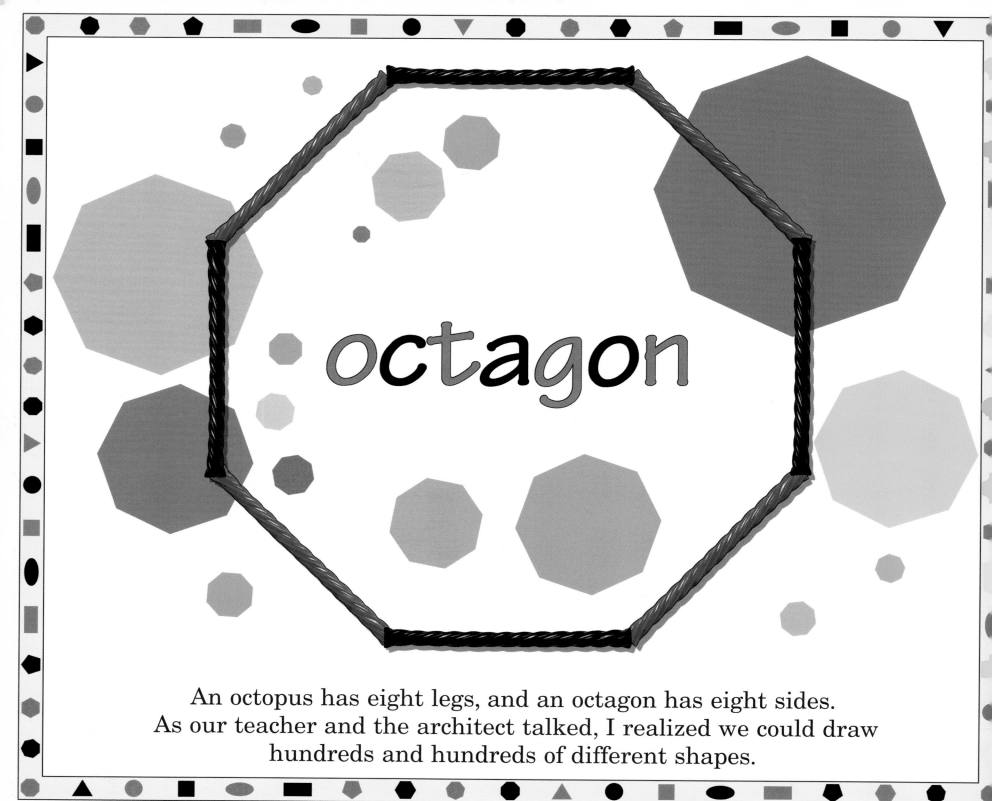

octagon

An octopus has eight legs, and an octagon has eight sides.
As our teacher and the architect talked, I realized we could draw
hundreds and hundreds of different shapes.

A nonagon has nine sides. Our whole class tried to think of a nonagon in our town or near our school. We couldn't think of any. Maybe for homework, our parents can help us find one.

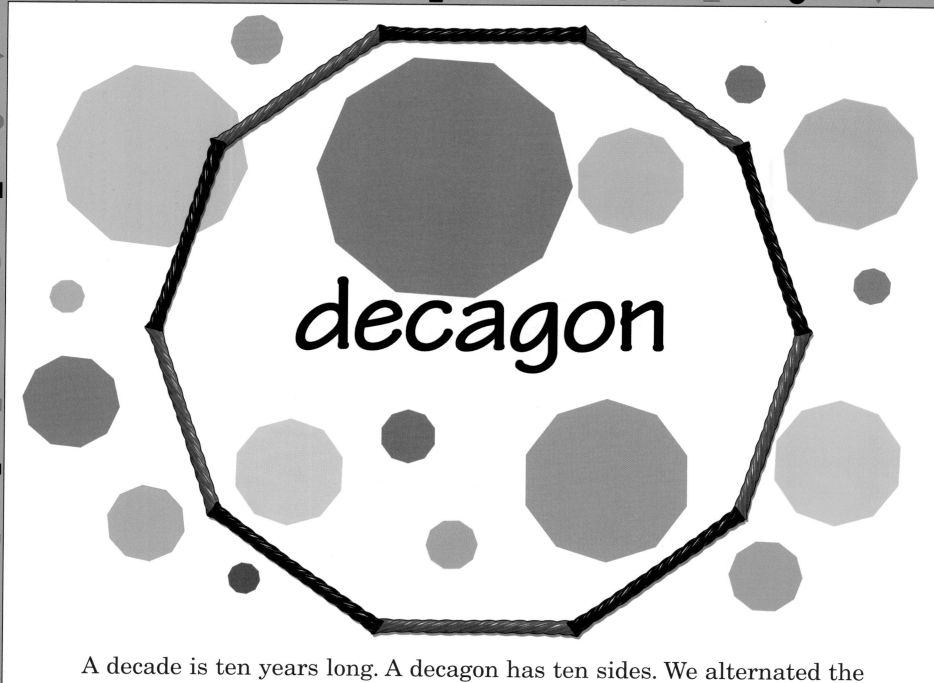

decagon

A decade is ten years long. A decagon has ten sides. We alternated the flavors — strawberry, licorice, strawberry, licorice, strawberry, licorice — to make this shape. Our teacher told us we were making a pattern.

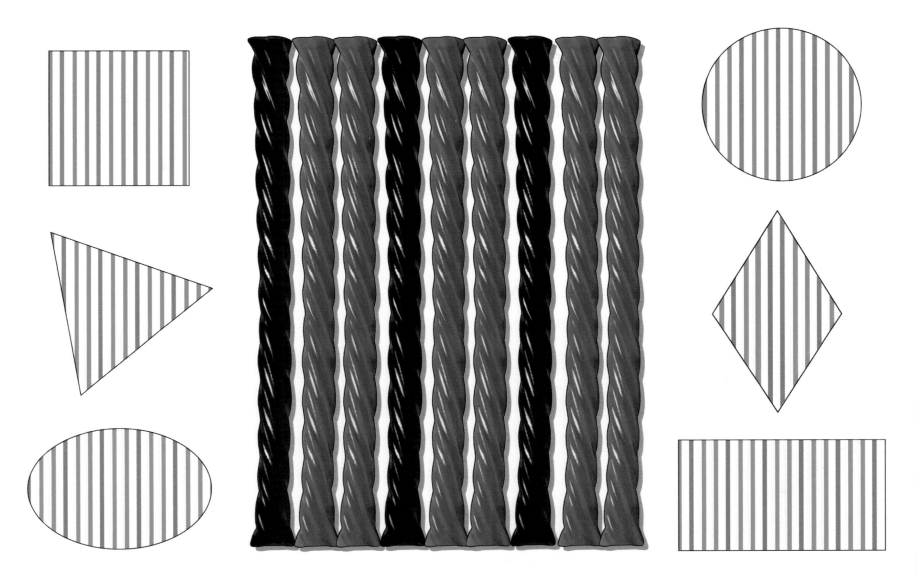

Here is another pattern. One black candy, two red candies, one black, two red, one black, two red. All but one of the patterns on this page go "one, two, one, two." Can you find the different pattern on this page?

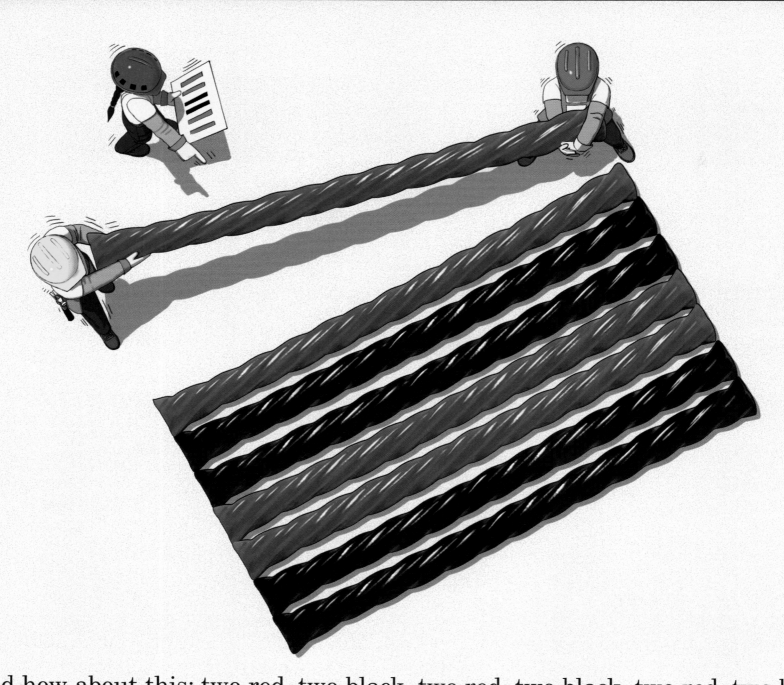

And how about this: two red, two black, two red, two black, two red, two black.
I guess you could call it a "two-two" pattern.

I like this pattern the best: three red, one black, three red, one black, three red. Or you could call this pattern: three strawberry, one licorice, three strawberry, one licorice, three strawberry. And what would come next? This is a "three-one" pattern.

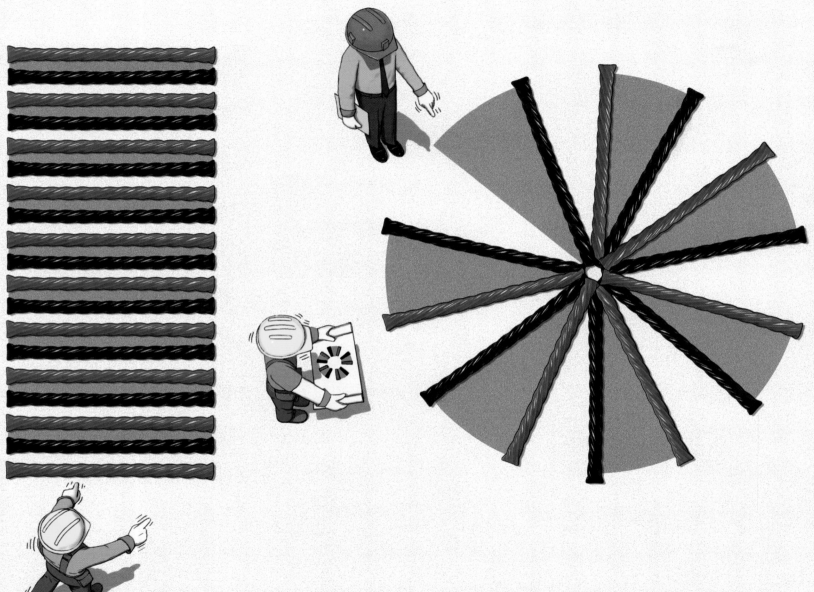

Here is one more pattern: one red candy, blue chalk,
one black candy, space. We made two shapes using this pattern.

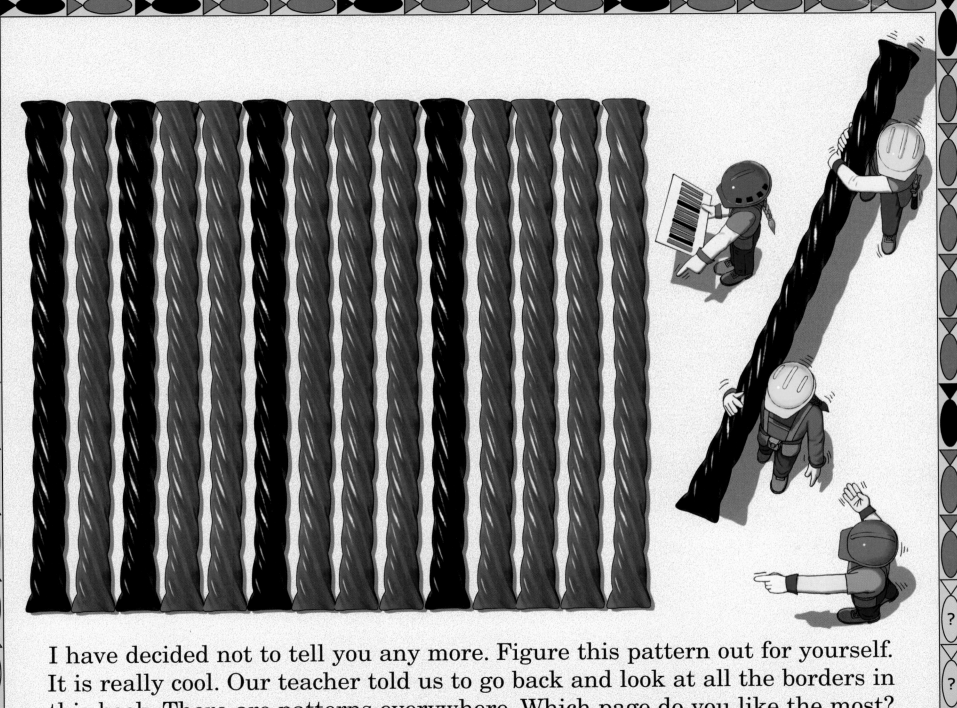

I have decided not to tell you any more. Figure this pattern out for yourself. It is really cool. Our teacher told us to go back and look at all the borders in this book. There are patterns everywhere. Which page do you like the most?

The architect says we did a great job learning our shapes.
My teacher says I am a star! I thought about it. I am really
five triangles with a pentagon in the middle!